better together*

*This book is best read together, grownup and kid.

 akidsco.com

a
kids
book
about

a kids book about

LONG-TERM CARE

by Jenny Abeling
illustrated by Mary Matthews

a kids book about

Text and design copyright © 2024
by A Kids Book About, Inc.

Copyright is good! It ensures that work like this can exist, and more work in the future can be created.

All rights reserved. No part of this publication may be reproduced, distributed, or transmitted in any form or by any means, including photocopying, recording, other electronic or mechanical methods, without the prior written permission of the publisher, except in the case of brief quotations embodied in critical reviews and certain other noncommercial uses permitted by copyright law. For permission requests, write to the publisher.

A Kids Book About, Kids Are Ready, and the colophon 'a' are trademarks of A Kids Book About, Inc.

Printed in the United States of America.

A Kids Book About books are available online: *akidsco.com*

To share your stories, ask questions, or inquire about bulk purchases (schools, libraries, and nonprofits), please use the following email address: *hello@akidsco.com*

Print ISBN: 979-8-89281-042-5
Ebook ISBN: 979-8-89281-043-2

Designed by Rick DeLucco
Edited by Jennifer Goldstein and Emma Wolf

To my original caregivers, my family, and to all the caregivers across the world who show up every day and care for their communities.

Intro

A *Kids Book About Long-Term Care* is all about helping young readers understand what long-term care is and why it matters. Long-term care may sound complex, but we're here to break it down in a way that's easy to understand.

In these pages, we'll explore what long-term care means, why it's important, and how it connects us across generations. We'll learn how caring for our elderly and disabled family members and friends isn't just an obligation—it's an act of love that makes our communities stronger.

A Kids Book About Long-Term Care is your guide to understanding the importance of caring for and learning from aged and disabled individuals, preserving intergenerational bonds, and making our world a kinder place for everyone, regardless of age or ability. Let's embark on this adventure together and explore the beauty of caring across generations.

DO YOU KNOW ANYONE WHO'S RECEIVING LONG-TERM CARE?

LONG-TERM CARE is support provided by people who are specially trained to help other people meet their care needs every day.

LONG-TERM CARE is for people with physical or developmental needs, as well as people who require mental and emotional help.

LONG-TERM CARE can be for kids, elders, grownups, extended family members, teachers, neighbors—pretty much anyone!

The goal of long-term care
is to promote each person's

INDEPENDENCE, DIGNITY, AND FREEDOM OF CHOICE.

What can long-term care look like?

HERE ARE SOME EXAMPLES...

A grandparent who has dementia lives with you at home and your parents are their caregivers.

One of your classmates has physical or developmental* disabilities and has a service provider who helps support them throughout the day.

Your aunt had hip surgery and needs to recover at a rehabilitation center to learn how to safely move around in a walker or wheelchair.

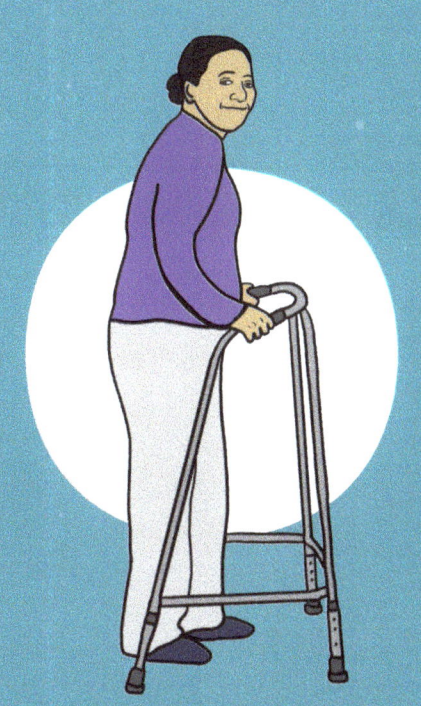

Your neighbor has a caregiver who supports their mental and emotional health needs by advocating for them and helping with medical appointments.

*Developmental disabilities are a group of conditions due to an impairment in physical, learning, language, or behavior areas. These conditions begin during the developmental period, may impact day-to-day functioning, and usually last throughout a person's lifetime.

People can receive care in:

- **THEIR HOME**

- **GROUP HOMES**

- **COMMUNITY-BASED PROGRAMS**

- **ASSISTED LIVING FACILITIES**

- **MEMORY CARE FACILITIES**

- **NURSING HOMES**

- **REHABILITATION CENTERS**

Caregivers and service providers help support **ACTIVITIES OF DAILY LIVING,** or ADL's, for the people in their care.

What are ADL's?

The things we need every day like:

 **COOKING MEALS AND EATING,**

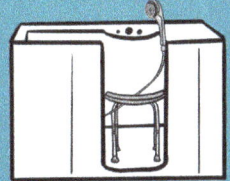 **TAKING A BATH OR SHOWER,**

 **GETTING IN AND OUT OF BED,**

 **GETTING DRESSED,**

BRUSHING HAIR,

BRUSHING TEETH,

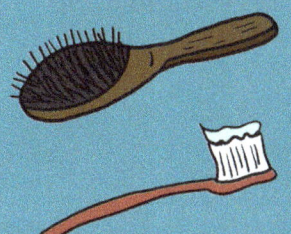 **ORGANIZING AND TAKING MEDICATIONS,**

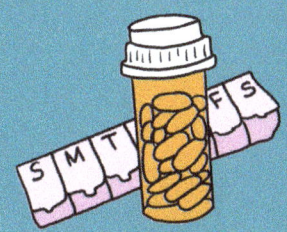 **GETTING TO APPOINTMENTS OR SEEING HEALTHCARE PROFESSIONALS.**

At some point, everyone will need some kind of long-term care support.

YES, EVERYONE!

So, it's important we all understand what it is.

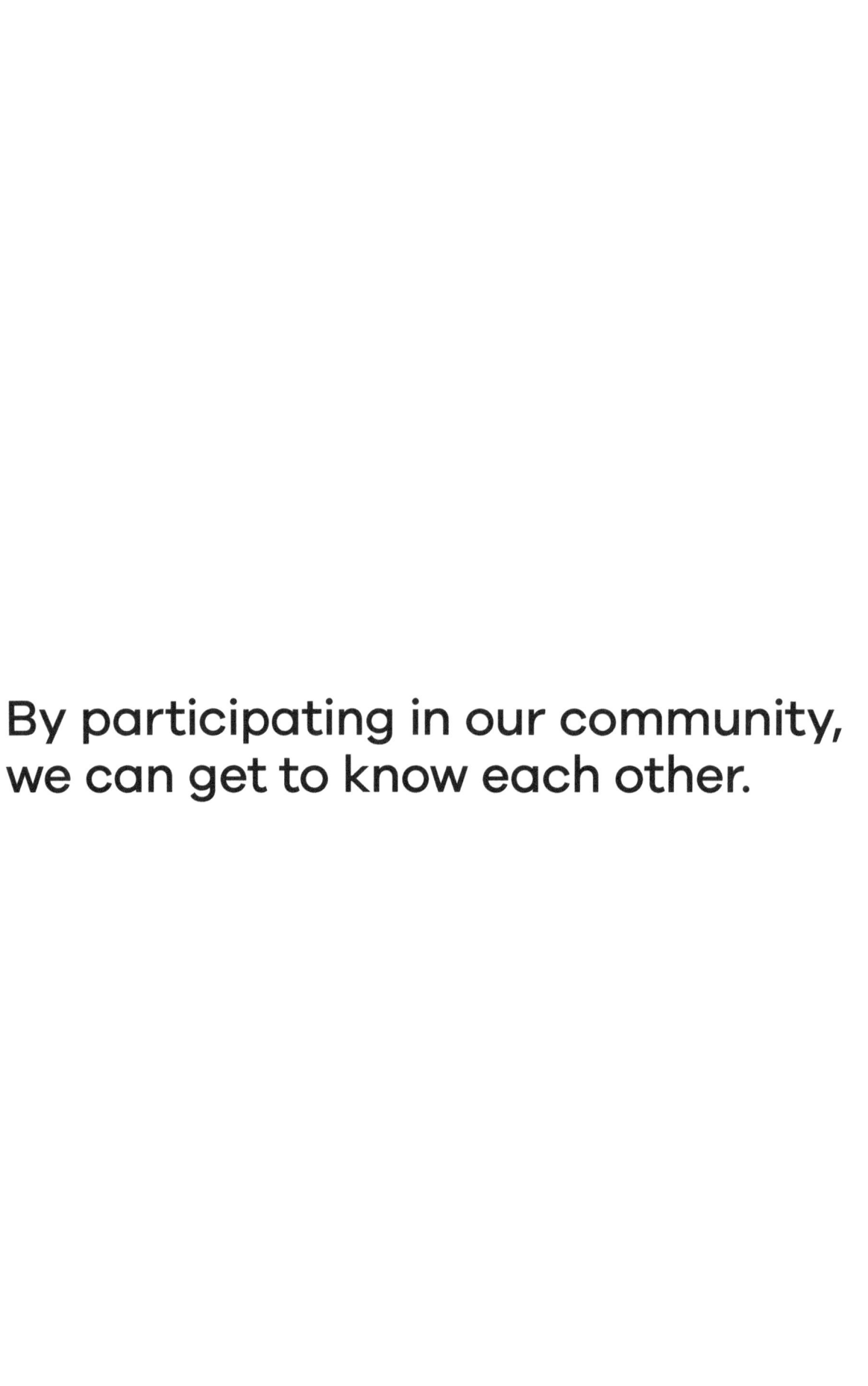

By participating in our community, we can get to know each other.

AND GUESS WHAT?

I bet there are lots of people in your own community who receive some of these services.

One important part of being in a community is learning about everyone's different needs.

Sometimes that involves building intergenerational* relationships where people of different ages and abilities come together to support and lift each other up.

*Intergenerational relationships are those formed between individuals of different generations. Some examples include a parent and kid, an elder and a grownup, or a grandparent and a grandkid.

THESE BONDS
STRENG
COMMU

THEN OUR
NITIES.

We grow when we share
and learn from one another.

We strengthen our communities
when we share our talents and
abilities so that we all thrive
and are stronger together.

Everyone has a skill or life experience*
that can be shared across generations.

*Life experience is knowledge and/or
perspective gained just by being alive!

FOR EXAMPLE, GRANDPARENTS PASS DOWN CULTURAL COOKING TRADITIONS TO THEIR KIDS AND GRANDCHILDREN.

KIDS ASSIST THEIR ELDERS WITH TECHNOLOGY TO HELP US ALL STAY CONNECTED.

INDIVIDUALS WITH DISABILITIES TEACH TOLERANCE, COMPASSION, AND PATIENCE THROUGH THEIR LIVED EXPERIENCE.

People don't always get enough support and services, which can be hard and may cause them to feel

UNSEEN OR UNHEARD.

IT'S OUR JOB AS COMMUNITY MEMBERS TO INCLUDE A

LEARNING ABOUT LONG-TERM CARE EMPOWERS THE PEOPLE WHO NEED IT.

It also empowers kids and families to better navigate transitions for their loved ones.

We often learn about long-term care when someone we know gets sick or ends up in the hospital.

But what if we learned more about it now, so we're all better prepared?

THAT COULD MAKE THE EXPERIENCE LESS SCARY AND LESS STRESSFUL.

We also need more people to do this important work, and there are all types of jobs!

CAREGIVERS and **SERVICE PROVIDERS** to take care of those in need.

CERTIFIED NURSING ASSISTANTS (CNAs) to help with ADL's.

NURSES to help keep folks healthy.

MEDICATION AIDES to help patients take the right medicine.

DIETARY STAFF provide nourishment to people.

JANITORIAL STAFF to help keep things clean and sanitary.

SOCIAL WORKERS, CASE MANAGERS, and **THERAPY STAFF** to help with physical, behavioral, occupational, or speech needs.

And guess what?

The most important skills you need, you already have.

IT'S TRUE!

Anyone with a caring heart and a desire to help others can learn to be a caregiver.

The long-term care field
can be a great place to work!

We have a diverse group of individuals who need long-term care—people of different races, genders, ethnicities, and ages—so we need workers who can meet those needs.

AND THAT COULD BE YOU.

Now that you have all this information, go out and share it!

Start a conversation about long-term care with someone today.

GO OUT INTO YOUR COMMUNITY AND CREATE BONDS WITH PEOPLE WHO NEED LONG-TERM CARE SUPPORT.

LOOK FOR VOLUNTEER OPPORTUNITIES WITH YOUR FAMILY AND FRIENDS!

Talk to your teachers and neighbors about creating new connections with people who utilize long-term care.

It's up to all of us to build stronger relationships with those in our communities, regardless of age or ability.

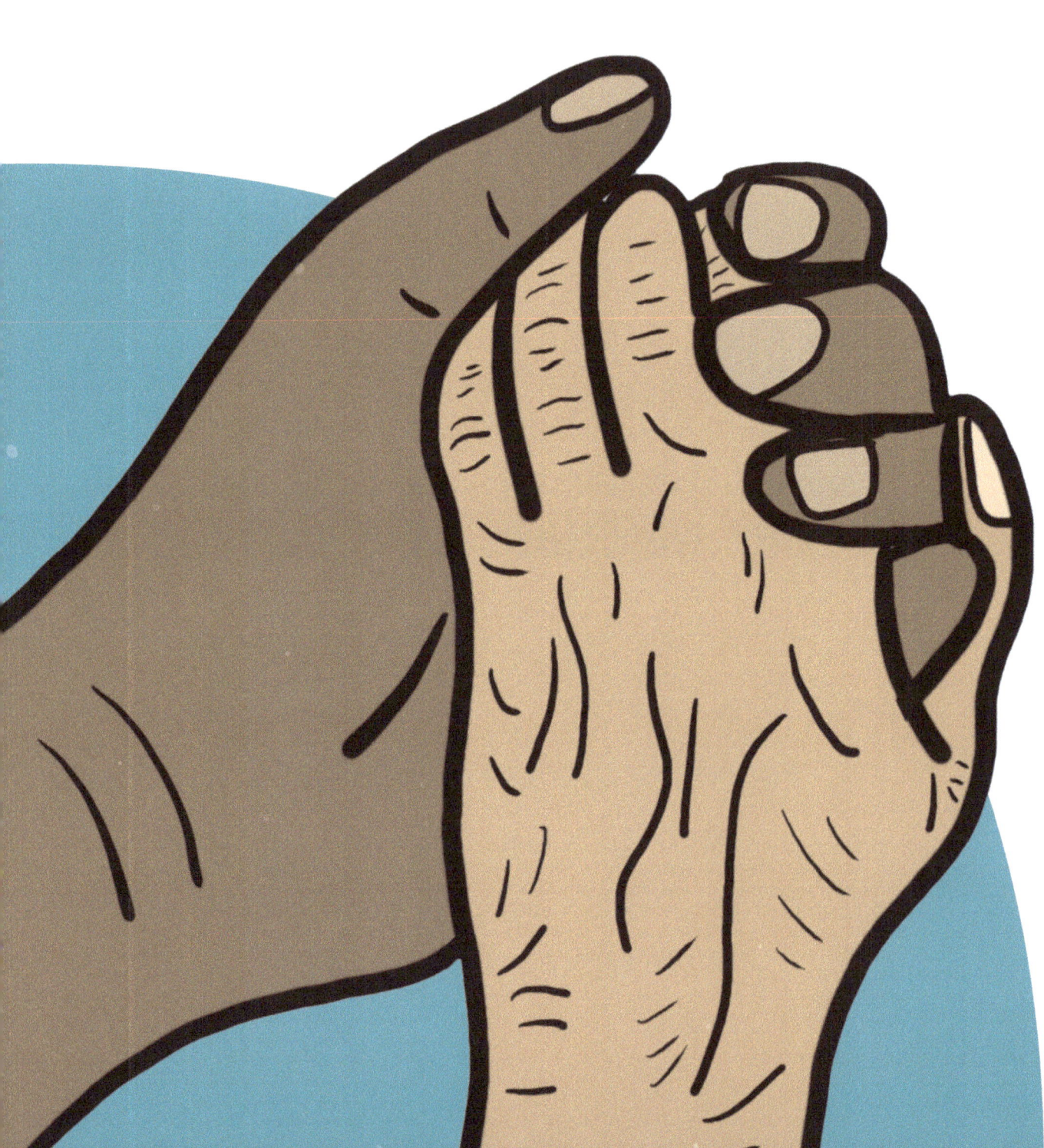

AND YOU CAN START THAT TODAY!

Resources

Caring Across Generations
caringacross.org
Caring Across Generations is a movement of family caregivers, care workers, disabled people, and aging adults working to transform care across the lifespan so it's accessible, affordable, and equitable—and enables everyone to live and age with dignity.

Teepa Snow
teepasnow.com
Teepa Snow is an Occupational Therapist with over forty years of experience related to supporting those living with brain change. She founded Positive Approach to Care, an organization that provides education and products dedicated to improving awareness of dementia and other neurodiverse conditions. Teepa believes that educating children and teens about brain change is key to helping build a more inclusive global community. To connect with Teepa, please email info@teepasnow.com.

National Consumer Voice for Long-Term Care
theconsumervoice.org
The National Consumer Voice for Quality Long-Term Care (Consumer Voice) advocates for people needing long-term care— so that they can access services, get quality care and quality of life, and that their rights are respected.

SEIU
seiu.org
The Service Employees International Union (SEIU) represents more than 2 million workers across the country, including more than 1 million healthcare workers, such as doctors, nurses, hospital workers, home care workers, and nursing home workers. Together, SEIU members are advocating for higher wages and a union for all workers, and are working to build a future where everyone can access and afford the care they need, no matter the color of their skin, the language they speak, or where they live.

Bridge Meadows
bridgemeadows.org
Bridge Meadows believes in a world where all generations are cherished. When people live together in community, relationships are built, creating safety nets of support for the well-being of the whole community. A Bridge Meadows community provides permanency of home and family for children and youth who have been impacted by foster care. Bridge Meadows is not just a place where people live—it is a place where people find connection, purpose, and family.

Outro

Though this book is coming to a close, we hope the conversation continues. Long-term care might seem like a grownup topic, but it's essential for everyone, no matter their age or abilities, to understand the importance of caring for one another.

Maybe you're thinking, how do I get more involved in long-term care and the communities which support people who need it? Great question! Check out our long-term care resources page and explore the advocacy and educational organizations with the people you know.

The values of compassion, empathy, and understanding make our world a better place. And just as the seeds you plant today will grow into mighty trees, the love and care you share now will make our world more loving and cared for.

Know that you are the future, and the future is full of love, care, and inclusion for all.

About the Author & Illustrator

Jenny Abeling's (she/her) inspiration for this book took root amid the height of the COVID-19 pandemic. In those trying times, she felt a profound urge to champion the cause of long-term care consumers and workers.

Jenny joined forces with illustrator and cartoonist Mary Matthews (she/her) to help bring the faces and personalities of long-term care to life.

They want to create pathways for kids and families to engage with long-term care, fostering intergenerational spaces for mutual learning and growth, and confronting the pervasive issues of ageism and ableism deeply entrenched in our society.

 @galpalmedia    @galpalmedia

 www.galpalproductions.com

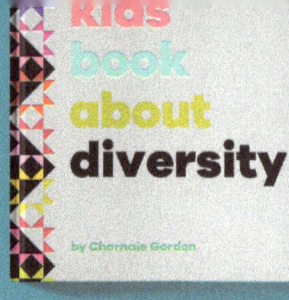

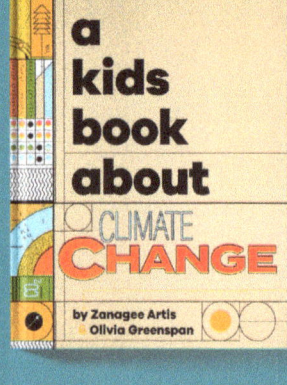

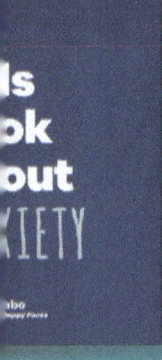

www.ingramcontent.com/pod-product-compliance
Lightning Source LLC
Chambersburg PA
CBHW061359010526
44107CB00012B/989